# DATE DUE

| | | | |
|---|---|---|---|
| NOV 6 '92 | | | |
| JAN 6 1994 | | | |
| APR 20 1994 | | | |
| | | | |
| | | | |
| | | | |
| | | | |
| | | | |
| | | | |
| | | | |
| | | | |
| | | | |
| | | | |
| | | | |

# A McGRAW-HILL NEW BIOLOGY

*Scientific Adviser : Dr. Gwynne Vevers*
*Curator of the Aquarium and Invertebrates,*
*The Zoological Society of London*

## OWLS

## OTHER BOOKS IN THIS SERIES

*Chimpanzees*
Prue Napier, illustrated by Douglas Bowness

*Fishes*
Gwynne Vevers, illustrated by Alan Jessett

*Frogs, Toads & Newts*
F. D. Ommanney, illustrated by Deborah Fulford

*Spiders & Scorpions*
J. L. Cloudsley-Thompson, illustrated by Joyce Bee

*Bees & Wasps*
J. L. Cloudsley-Thompson, illustrated by Joyce Bee

*Crocodiles & Alligators*
J. L. Cloudsley-Thompson, illustrated by Joyce Bee

*Birds of Prey that hunt by day*
Clive Catchpole, illustrated by David Nockels

A McGRAW-HILL NEW BIOLOGY

*Clive Catchpole*

# Owls

*Illustrated by David Nockels*

# McGRAW-HILL BOOK COMPANY

*New York   St. Louis   San Francisco*

# Metric Conversion Table

1 centimeter = 0.39 inch
1 meter = 3.27 feet
1 kilometer = 0.62 mile

1 sq. centimeter = 0.15 sq. inch
1 sq. meter = 10.76 sq. feet
1 hectare = 2.47 acres
1 sq. kilometer = 0.39 sq. mile

1 kilogram = 2.21 lb (avoirdupois)
1 tonne = 0.98 (long) ton

**Library of Congress Cataloging in Publication Data**

Catchpole, Clive.
  Owls.
  (McGraw-Hill new biology series)
  Includes index.
  SUMMARY: Describes the physical characteristics
and habits of various types of owls from different
parts of the world.
    1. Owls—Juvenile literature.
[1. Owls] 1. Nockels, David.
II. Title.
QL696.S83C37 1977     598.9'7     77–8371
ISBN 0–07–010232–5 lib. bdg.

OWLS

First distribution in the United States of America
by McGraw-Hill Book Company, 1977.
Text © Clive Catchpole 1976.
Illustrations © David Nockels 1976.
First printed in Great Britain for
The Bodley Head
by William Clowes & Sons Ltd., Beccles
*First published 1976*

# Contents

1. Introduction   7

2. What are owls?   9

3. Breeding behavior   16

4. Barn and bay owls   26

5. Scops and screech owls   29

6. Eagle owls and the Snowy Owl   32

7. Fish and hawk owls   36

8. Little and pygmy owls   40

9. Wood and eared owls   43

   Index   47

Great Grey Owl
(0·7 m.)

Bay Owl (0·25 m.)

Ferruginous Pygmy Owl (0·2 m.)

Different types and sizes of owls. The measurement given for each bird is the approximate length in meters from beak to tail.

# 1

# Introduction

Birds belong to a group of animals which have one thing in common, they all have a backbone. Many other animals, including mammals, reptiles, amphibians and fishes, share this important characteristic with birds. The backbone is made up of tiny bones called vertebrae, and so these animals are called "vertebrates." You can feel the knobbly vertebrae which make up your backbone, for human beings are vertebrates, too.

What makes birds different from other vertebrates are their feathers. Feathers are very special structures indeed. No other animal group has them and so birds are unique in this respect. In other ways birds resemble reptiles, and many millions of years ago developed from reptile ancestors. You can still see the horny, reptile-like scales on their legs, and the laying of eggs is really a reptilian habit.

The feathers birds have developed are important in two ways. They help to keep the body warm, for birds, like mammals, are "warm-blooded" and maintain a high body temperature. This is the chief reason why birds can keep active throughout the cold, winter months when "cold-blooded" animals become inactive, or even hibernate. Larger, special feathers on the wings and tail are the reason why birds can fly with such effortless grace, something which few other vertebrates can do. Owls, like most birds, are superb fliers, but unusual in one respect. They fly and hunt by night, on large, silent wings.

Long-eared Owl (0·4 m.)

Great Horned Owl (0·5 m.)

8

White-faced Scops Owl (0·2 m.)

# 2

# What are owls?

Of all birds, owls are probably the most instantly recognizable. There is something about their shape which makes them look quite different from other birds. The most striking feature is the large head with two enormous, staring eyes set close together. The head seems to merge into the rather bulky body when the owl perches upright. No wonder that to many people owls have an almost human appearance, both comic and appealing. Whatever the reasons, owls have a very special place in our stories and legends and are usually regarded as being elderly, sober, kind and wise. But there is also a darker side to owls, and one which is much nearer the truth. In horror films and ghost stories, at the most sinister moment, a close-up of those wide, staring eyes or the eerie hoot of an owl is enough to send shivers down the spine. For owls are hunting creatures of the night, and almost all their special features have developed to make them efficient at finding and killing their prey in the dark.

Owls are not the only birds which hunt and kill fairly large animals. Like birds of prey they have powerful talons for killing and special hooked beaks for tearing flesh, but true birds of prey, such as eagles and falcons, hunt by day and are called the

Falconiformes. Owls are nocturnal, hunting by night, and so are classified by zoologists in a separate group of their own called the Strigiformes. It is not true that all owls hunt only by night, but most do, though a few hunt by day.

The powerful talons of the Eurasian Eagle Owl.

It is also not true that owls can see in complete darkness. In a lightproof room or a deep cave, where it is completely dark, an owl would not see any more than a human being. But even at night it is never completely dark out of doors; there is always some light, particularly from the stars and moon. The eyes of an owl are designed to collect and respond to what little light there is at dusk and through the night. The eyes are extremely large, to collect as much light as possible. At night the iris opens as far

10

Day                    Night

The eye of the Eurasian Eagle Owl by day and by night.

as it can, creating an enormous pupil to let in more light. The light passes through the lens right to the back of the eye onto the retina. In owls the retina contains large numbers of special cells called rods. Rods are particularly sensitive to dim light, and animals which have large numbers of them in the retina are able to see much better at night.

It is also untrue that owls are blind in daylight, for some even hunt by day. But the large sensitive eyes need protection from bright light. This is achieved mainly by closing the iris and leaving only a tiny pupil which hardly lets in any light.

The position of the eyes is also important. Set close together, their fields of vision overlap and so give binocular vision. This means that owls are very

Tawny Owl on silent wings by night.
(Wing-span about 0·8 m.)

good at judging depth and distance, which is important for an animal hunting moving prey. The curious head-bobbing movements owls make when staring at an object also help to judge distance accurately. Because of the position and tubular shape of the eyes, owls cannot move them to see to the side or behind. Instead, due to a very flexible neck, they can move the whole head almost completely around.

Owls also have large, well-developed ears, but these are not so easily seen. The feathery "ear tufts" on the heads of many owls have nothing to do with hearing, but are used for visual signaling. Equally, the large "facial discs" of feathers around the eyes have nothing to do with seeing. It is thought that somehow they deflect sounds towards the ears which lie behind. The real ear openings are large slits underneath the feathers on each side of the head, and are usually protected by ear flaps and feathers. The ears are extremely sensitive and can detect the tiny, high-pitched squeaks and rustlings made by small rodents as they scuttle along at night. To many owls, ears are just as important as eyes for hunting. In complete darkness a Barn Owl can locate and catch a mouse, so long as the mouse moves or squeaks occasionally.

When hunting by sound, it is important to be as silent as possible in flight. Rodents also have acute powers of hearing, and if they hear the swish of large wings will soon find a safe hiding place. Also, the tiny rodent sounds the owl is listening for might easily be drowned by its own noise. So owls have developed the remarkable ability to fly silently, which makes their sudden appearance in the night even more ghostly and much more dangerous. Silent flight is achieved in two ways. First, owls have very large wings in relation to their weight. They are made to seem larger than they are by their loose, fluffy plumage covering a body which is much thinner than it looks. Having large wings and small bodies means that owls need to flap much less, can fly more slowly, and are also very maneuverable.

Barn Owl at the kill.

Secondly, the wing feathers are specially designed to be silent as they move against the air. Instead of being stiff, they are soft, almost furry, and fringed at the edges. This seems to lessen the noise as they beat through the air.

Most owls hunt low over open ground on silent wings, or sit on a perch watching and listening for small rodents or other animals active by night. Whichever way the owl hunts, by sight, sound or both, the end for the victim is much the same. The owl descends onto its prey feet first and kills with its large, razor-sharp talons. Two toes face forward and two backward and the prey is either pierced or crushed to death. The prey may be swallowed whole or carried away in the beak or talons. Although to us owls may appear amusing or cuddly, in nature they are predators, silent and deadly hunters of the night.

Soft, fringed flight feather of the Tawny Owl.

**3**

# Breeding behavior

Most owls breed in the spring and stay in the same area all year. The Tawny Owl is one of those, but some owls travel great distances to spend the winter in warmer areas where food is more plentiful. This is called migration. The European Scops Owl migrates from Europe each year to spend the winter in North Africa. Whether migratory or not, the birds tend to return each year to breed in the very same place, and this is called their territory. A territory is the name given to the piece of land which

Threat display of male Tawny Owl
near the nest hole.

each breeding pair will nest in and jealously guard against all other members of the same species. The males in particular will fight viciously to defend their territories, especially near the nest. Owl territories vary in size, but may contain many square kilometers within their boundaries.

Because they are active by night, owls have developed elaborate ways of communicating by voice. Perhaps the best known is the hoot of the Tawny Owl, usually described as "tu-whit tu-whoo." As well as hoots, other owl noises have been described as screeches, screams, chimes, snores and coughs. They are particularly useful for communication over long distances at night, and one important function is to proclaim ownership of a territory. The piercing cries carry long distances on the night air, across open country or woodland, and warn rival males to keep well away. When they are nearer to each other owls may use visual communication in the form of a threat display. Then the feathers are fluffed up and the wings extended to make the owl seem much bigger and more frightening to his rivals. The bill may be opened and shut to make a snapping noise, and the owl may move menacingly from one foot to the other as though about to attack. Displays in birds are really a simple type of sign language which they all understand. Here the message is unmistakable—"keep out or I will attack!"

The territory should contain a good supply of prey to feed a whole family of owls as well as places to nest and roost in the daytime. Roosting is when the owls rest or sleep and perhaps digest the prey eaten during a busy night of hunting. As they roost in the daytime, the roost must be a safe, secluded place such as a crevice, hole or leafy branch. Owls are often camouflaged with dull, streaky plumage which blends into the background. They also keep very still and so stand a good chance of not being seen. But if they are seen by small birds, such as finches and tits, their characteristic shape is instantly recognized. The small birds give special

18

alarm calls which warn others that an owl has been discovered nearby. They seem to know that the owl is less dangerous by day and join in to "mob" the sleepy owl by flying and scolding around it in large numbers. Small birds are so attracted to mob an owl that hundreds are caught by human hunters using stuffed owls to lure them to be shot or trapped.

The hoots and screeches of the male are also used to attract a female to his territory for pairing. Once paired, owls may stay together for many years or even life. Before breeding begins there is usually a period of display. Sexual displays look rather like threat displays, but this time they are a way of making sure the pair are ready and willing to mate. In Tawny Owls the male may fluff up his feathers and spread his wings in a way similar to a threat display, but he also makes swaying and bobbing movements. In some species the male may present the female with a tasty item of prey he has caught. When the female indicates she is ready, the male hops onto her back to mate. To do so before this

Small birds "mobbing" a sleepy Little Owl.

would be dangerous, as in most owls the female is larger than the male. The external sex organs are similar and the two openings are pressed together. The male discharges sperm into the female and quickly hops off. The female is now capable of laying fertilized eggs, but first a nesting place must be found.

Owls hardly ever build their own nests. One of the few species which occasionally does is the giant Great Grey Owl of Europe, Asia and North America, but the nest, placed high in a tree, is only an ugly, clumsy pile of twigs. Most owls, like the Tawny Owl, find a hole in a large tree where they are safe from other predators searching for eggs or young. As well as holes in rotten trees, owls use the holes made by woodpeckers in previous years. The tiny Elf Owl in North America uses holes made by woodpeckers in the giant cactus forests of the desert, which are well protected by sharp spines. Some owls use the old, abandoned nests of other birds. The Long-eared Owl of Europe, Asia and North America frequently uses the nests of crows, magpies and jays. A few owls live in open country where there are no trees and so are forced to nest on the ground. The Short-eared Owl hunts over open grassland in Europe, Asia and the Americas. The nest is just a shallow depression on the ground some-times lined with grasses. Perhaps the most curious nesting place is that of the Burrowing Owl from the

The female Long-eared Owl is incubating, while
the male perches nearby.

Newly hatched young and eggs of Short-eared
Owl in nest on the ground.

prairies of North America. As its name suggests, it nests in burrows underground. Although the owl can dig out a burrow, it usually occupies the burrows of other animals, such as Prairie Dogs.

Owls usually lay between two and four eggs, but some lay many more. The eggs are different from those of many birds as they are almost completely round and perfectly white. In most other birds the eggs are pear-shaped, which stops them rolling out of the nest, but in hole-nesting species the eggs are safe from falling out and so can be rounded in shape. In holes the eggs are hidden from predators and so there is no need for camouflage by colored blotches or speckles.

In order to develop and hatch, the eggs must be incubated, which means keeping them as near to body temperature as possible. To do this the larger female owl sits on them and the incubation period may last from three to five weeks. During this time the smaller male hunts and brings food to the female on the nest. Eggs may be laid at intervals several

22

days apart. As incubation starts with the very first egg, the owlets hatch out at intervals. This means that in the nest the young are all different sizes. In good years when food is plentiful all the young owlets may survive, but in bad years when food is scarce, the older, larger ones take it all and the smaller ones starve to death. This seems very cruel, but is nature's way of ensuring that even in poor years at least one or two young will grow strong enough to survive and carry on the species. If all the young shared the small amount of food equally, then none might survive.

When the young are hatched the female will still stay with them while the male now hunts for all the family. As 'they grow bigger the female may also

A parent brings food to young Barn Owls
of different sizes.

hunt to provide more food. Newly hatched owlets may have the food prepared for them by having the limbs and head removed. Barn Owls bring smaller prey such as voles and mice to young owlets, but as they grow older larger animals such as rats are brought.

One way of discovering what prey is being caught and eaten is to study owl pellets. Owls often swallow their prey whole and take in large amounts of indigestible fur, feathers and bones. These are formed into a pellet in the gizzard and regurgitated by special pumping movements of the head and neck. Large numbers of pellets can be found near nests and roosting sites, and by examining their contents of bones, teeth and other hard parts it is possible to identify the prey eaten. In England, Barn Owls hunting over open country leave pellets which contain large numbers of Short-tailed Voles, common inhabitants of grassland. Tawny Owls hunting through the normal woodland habitat leave pellets containing mainly Wood Mice and Bank Voles. The same species hunting through the parks of central London leave pellets containing mainly the smaller birds which breed there: House Sparrows, European Blackbirds, Starlings and even pigeons. The size, shape, color and texture of pellets can be used to identify the species of owl which made them. Generally, the smaller the owl the smaller the pellet and Barn Owl pellets are smaller, darker and more shiny than those of the Tawny Owl.

Eventually the young become fully grown and must leave the nest. Only by much practice will they learn to fly and hunt like their parents, and even after leaving the nest they may still be fed by their parents until well into autumn. Not many will survive the first winter to breed the next spring, but owls live for many years and only a few are needed each year to ensure that the species survives.

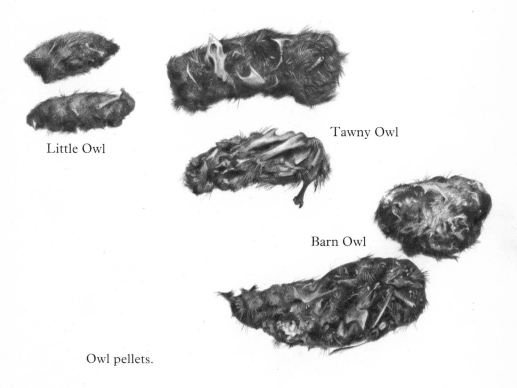

Little Owl

Tawny Owl

Barn Owl

Owl pellets.

# 4

# Barn and bay owls

Barn owls are probably the best-known group of owls. The most common species, the Barn Owl, is found in every continent except Antarctica. The upper parts are orange-brown, but the characteristic heart-shaped face and underparts are white and make it a most conspicuous bird in flight. It is usually seen at dusk and often picked out in the beam of car headlights on country roads. The white, silent, ghost-like appearance of the Barn Owl is sometimes enhanced by a visible glow reported by some observers. This may be due to luminous bacteria deposited on the feathers from the decaying

Barn Owl hunting over farmland at night.
(Wing-span about 0·8 m.)

wood of roosting or nesting holes. The call of the Barn Owl is not a hoot, but a long, eerie shriek uttered on the wing. It is a bird of open country, hunting low over plains, moors or deserts.

In England the Barn Owl is associated with farmland, and as the name suggests, frequently occupies old barns. No nest is built, but the eggs are laid in some safe place. Church towers or any disused buildings which can provide a sheltered ledge may be used, but natural rock crevices or hollow trees are just as suitable. Small nocturnal rodents such as mice and voles are the chief prey, but small birds, bats, insects and even fish may be taken. By keeping down rodents on farms, the Barn Owl is probably beneficial to man, but has been persecuted by game-keepers and taxidermists in the past. Modern farming, with the removal of old farm buildings, the disappearance of hedgerows, and the use of poisonous insecticide sprays, may mean that this magnificent bird will be a less common sight over farmland in the future.

The Grass Owl is another type of barn owl found over much of the world. As its name suggests, it hunts over open grassland and also lays its eggs on the ground in a tussock of grass. In Australia, which has more types of barn owl than any other country, the Grass Owl feeds mainly on marsupial mice. The large Masked Owl of Tasmania hunts for larger prey such as rabbits, but also takes marsupial possums and rat-kangaroos.

The Bay Owl with insect prey.

Bay owls are a little-known group, rather mysterious but similar to barn owls in many ways. They share the heart-shaped face and like barn owls are believed to depend a good deal on hearing for finding their prey. Bay owls are different in that instead of hunting in open country, they live and hunt in dense, tropical jungle. One species, the Bay Owl, is found from India to Malaysia and feeds on a wide variety of small forest mammals, birds, reptiles, amphibians, fish and insects. Eggs are usually laid in a hollow tree. The African Bay Owl is the only other species, and even more retiring and elusive. One single specimen was discovered in 1951 near Lake Tanganyika, but no more have ever been caught.

# 5

# Scops and screech owls

Scops owls are found over most of Europe, Asia and Africa. The name is derived from the Greek *scopus* meaning "see" or "look at," presumably a reference to the large staring eyes set beneath conspicuous ear tufts. They are small, extremely attractive

The European Scops Owl is well camouflaged against the bark of a tree.

owls which hunt mainly for large insects. Their calls are very distinctive, consisting of a simple note repeated rather monotonously every few seconds. The European Scops Owl has a low, short whistle repeated every two seconds which is one of the most characteristic sounds of warm, summer nights in southern Europe. It inhabits fairly open woodland, orchards or olive groves and usually nests in tree holes. The European Scops Owl is a good example of camouflage, and it is extremely difficult to see even by day, as it remains very still. The beautifully marked plumage seems to blend into the very bark of the tree and the tiny owl merges completely into the background. At night it hunts for large insects such as crickets, grasshoppers, moths and beetles, but it occasionally may take small birds, rodents or lizards.

Common Screech Owl
pounces on a cricket.

Not all scops owls are so completely camouflaged. One of the most striking and attractive is the White-faced Scops Owl from Africa. It has large, orange eyes set into a conspicuous white face edged with black, and boldly striped body plumage.

Screech owls are found in North and South America. They are similar to scops owls in being small and feeding primarily on insects. The screech calls, which give them their name, are longer and more complicated than those of scops owls. The Common Screech Owl of North America is unusual in that there are two different colored forms, grey and red. It was thought at first that these were quite different species. The Common Screech Owl is found in woodland areas and nests in tree holes. The area around the nest is defended vigorously by these pugnacious little birds, and even human beings will be attacked if they venture too close. In summer, insects are the main prey, but in winter, unlike the European Scops Owl which migrates, the Common Screech Owl attempts to survive in the same areas now almost devoid of insect prey. It may have to hunt small mammals and birds, but some really wise owls will have stored away surplus food in their roosting sites. Food is also stored inside the body as fat, and by remaining safe, warm and inactive in their roosting sites many owls will survive the harsh Canadian winter, and emerge to breed in the spring.

# 6

# Eagle owls and the Snowy Owl

Eagle owls are some of the largest and probably the most magnificent of all owls. Their extremely large size and conspicuous ear tufts make them easy to recognize, and they usually have loud, hooting calls. As the name suggests, eagle owls are really the nocturnal equivalent of large birds of prey such as eagles which hunt by day. They are strong, fierce birds which hunt for larger prey than most owls.

Eurasian Eagle Owl attacks a fox.
(Wing-span about 1·6 m.)

Great Horned Owl
with rabbit prey.
(Size about 0·5 m.
from beak to tail.)

The Eurasian Eagle Owl is one of the best known and is found from the Arctic Circle to the Sahara. It lives in all types of habitat from dense forest to open desert, and usually nests on open ground or rocky ledges. It is a powerful hunter and takes a wide variety of prey: hedgehogs, rats, lemmings, crows, snakes and frogs. Sometimes large, dangerous prey are taken, such as wild cats, foxes, buzzards and falcons or even small deer. At the sight of a perched eagle owl in daytime, many birds of prey will launch a frenzied attack. Tethered or stuffed eagle owls have actually been used as lures by human hunters for falcons and hawks.

In North and South America lives another eagle

Snowy Owls at the nest. (Size about 0·6 m. from
beak to tail.) The male has brought a lemming to
feed to the young owlets.

owl, the Great Horned Owl, named after its huge ear tufts. An enormous, fierce bird, it will take rabbits, geese and snakes, and attack anyone who approaches its nest in the trees. Africa has more eagle owls than anywhere else, the most powerful being the Milky Eagle Owl which hunts for bush-babies, guinea fowl and bustard. Like all large eagle owls it is an awesome, fearful sight, particularly when seen fluffed up in a threat display. Its deep, hooting call is regarded as a bad omen by African tribesmen.

The beautiful Snowy Owl is closely related to eagle owls, and like them is extremely large. It hunts and breeds on the frozen Arctic tundra, but extends southwards to the Shetland Islands and Hudson Bay. Like Polar Bears and Arctic Foxes, the Snowy Owl is white and merges into the barren, white wilderness. The male is completely white, but the larger female is marked with narrow, brown bands. Snowy Owls nest on the ground and prefer a rocky vantage point from which to scan the vast, open tundra. In summer, living in the land of the midnight sun, the owls are forced to hunt a great deal by day. They hunt particularly for lemmings and hares, and the number of young they raise each year depends largely on whether it is a good or bad year for lemmings. Even though the parents are fierce defenders of the open nest, many owlets are lost to hungry Arctic Foxes and skuas.

# 7

# Fish and hawk owls

Fish owls are large, powerful owls which live by rivers and lakes in Africa and Asia. They resemble eagle owls, but hunt for fish, and so are really the nocturnal equivalent of the Osprey and fish eagles which hunt by day. Hunting for fish has meant that fish owls have developed special features to help in this difficult task. The feet are bare of feathers, and like those of the Osprey, are covered in sharp spines to help grip the slippery, wriggling prey. The talons themselves are long, curved and extremely sharp. Fish owls do not usually have the two important features found in eagle owls—facial discs and the ability to fly silently. Both of these are needed to hunt normal owl prey, but not fish. The fish below the water surface cannot hear the slight disturbance of wings in the air above, and so fish owls have no need for the soft plumage which gives silent flight. Fish are also hunted mainly by sight as they swim near the surface, so there is no need for facial discs which are thought to improve hearing.

Talons of Pel's Fishing Owl with spines
to grip slippery fish.

Malaysian Fish Owl with prey.

Boobook Owl with prey. A type of hawk owl
found in Australia and New Zealand.

Fish owls usually hunt from a perch overlooking the water below. When they see a fish near the surface they swoop down and snatch it up with their special feet. Although fish are the main prey, some fish owls such as the Malaysian Fish Owl will wade in shallow water searching for crayfish, crabs or frogs. Pel's Fishing Owl from Africa is one of the largest and most magnificent of all owls. It nests in tree holes close to rivers and has a deep, double hoot which carries far through the night jungle.

Hawk owls in many ways resemble hawks which hunt by day. They have the characteristic facial discs of owls but in a much reduced size, making the head seem smaller and more hawk-like. Like hawks they hunt mainly by sight, and some have long wings and tails. The Hawk Owl is found in northern parts of Europe, Asia and North America breeding mainly in coniferous forest. Unlike many owls, it does not fly silently, and indeed hunts mainly by day. It perches in a prominent position and swoops down to catch lemmings, voles, small birds and insects.

There are many large hawk owls in Australasia, perhaps because no eagle owls are found there. The Powerful Owl is the largest of them all and feeds mainly on marsupial possums and rabbits. The smaller Barking Owl feeds on small mammals, birds and insects. Its curious name derives from the distinctive double call which resembles a dog barking.

# 8

# Little and pygmy owls

This group contains the smallest of all the owls. Small, rounded and without ear tufts, these tiny owls are still efficient hunters both by day and night and can kill prey much larger than themselves. Although they take a wide variety of prey, insects are the most important food for many. The Little Owl is widespread over Europe, Asia and North Africa, and was introduced into Britain in the last century. It spread rapidly and was soon suspected of preying extensively on young game chicks and songbirds. A special inquiry using pellet analysis showed that throughout the year Little Owls fed mainly on insects but did take some small mammals and birds. The Little Owl nests in tree holes, but the Burrowing Owl of North and South America has the unusual habit of nesting underground. It can dig out its own burrows, but usually takes over those of plains-dwelling mammals such as prairie dogs. Active by day and night, the Burrowing Owl hunts across the open prairies for insects but can take rodents, birds and frogs.

Pygmy owls, as their name suggests, are even tinier. The Eurasian Pygmy Owl hunts through coniferous forests by day and night for a wide variety of prey: rodents, lizards, birds and insects.

Burrowing Owl at the entrance of a burrow.
(Size about 0·2 m. from beak to tail.)

A favorite nesting site is the disused hole of a woodpecker.

The minute Elf Owl is possibly the smallest owl in the world, only the size of a sparrow. It is found in the southwest United States and is well known for its habit of nesting in holes in giant cactus made by woodpeckers and flickers. The tiny Elf Owl emerges at dusk to hunt for insects which form its chief prey.

Elf Owl nesting in giant cactus.
(Size about 0·13 m. from beak to tail.)

# 9

# Wood and eared owls

Wood owls are quite large owls with big, round heads but no ear tufts. They have well-developed facial discs and rely mainly upon hearing to locate their prey at night. As their name suggests, wood owls breed and hunt almost always in woodland and nest mainly in tree holes. They are very fierce and have often attacked humans who approached too close to nests, causing serious injuries to the face with their sharp talons.

The Tawny Owl is one of the most common wood owls in Europe, Asia and North Africa. Although really an inhabitant of deciduous woodland, the Tawny Owl is surprisingly tolerant of man. It is even found breeding in central London where its beautiful, haunting cry drifts across the parks at night. Traditionally described as "tu-whit tu-whoo," it is perhaps more accurately written as "hoo-hoo-hoo-hoo-hooooooooooo," with a last, long, quavering note. The Tawny Owl rarely hunts before dark and takes a wide variety of prey: small mammals, birds, frogs, fish, insects and even earthworms. The giant Great Grey Owl is one of the largest of all owls and is found in the coniferous forests of northern Europe and North America. It is unusual among wood owls in never nesting in holes but instead using the abandoned nests of birds of prey. It is also unusual in frequently hunting by day for its main prey of voles.

Tawny Owl in London park.

Long-eared Owl.

Eared owls have ear tufts of various sizes, which may help them to recognize each other. The Long-eared Owl has extremely long and conspicuous ear tufts kept permanently raised, and also a pair of pale "eyebrows" set as if in a stern frown. It is found over much of the northern hemisphere, breeding in woodland and nesting mainly in abandoned nests of other birds such as crows or herons. By day it is extremely retiring and well camouflaged against the bark of trees. The prominent facial discs suggest that hearing is particularly important for hunting in the dark. Rodents form the main prey, but birds, bats, lizards, snakes and frogs are also taken.

The Short-eared Owl is found in South

America and many islands as well as in the northern hemisphere. It is an extremely successful hunter over open plains and marshes, and even nests on the open ground. The Short-eared Owl frequently hunts by day, and small mammals such as voles, shrews, rats and mice are its chief prey. It has been called the best mousetrap the farmer can have on his land. In years of rodent plagues, the Short-eared Owl may lay more eggs or even raise two broods instead of one. But in years of food shortage, the larger, stronger owlets in the brood will eat the smallest, so that some at least will survive to carry on the species. Even as a nestling, the amusing, cuddly owl begins to show the ruthless, killer instinct which is necessary for its own survival.

Short-eared Owl with mouse prey.

# Index

Barn owls, 26–8; Barn, 13, 14, 23, 26–7; Grass, 27; Masked, 27
Bay owls, 28; Bay, 6, 28; African Bay, 28
Beaks, 9
Breeding, 16–25

Camouflage, of eggs, 22; of plumage, 18, 29, 30, 31

Eagle owls, 32–3, 35; Eurasian Eagle, 10, 11, 32, 33; Great Horned, 8, 33, 35; Milky Eagle, 35
Eared owls, 45–6; Long-eared, 8, 20, 21, 45; Short-eared, 20, 22, 45–6
Ears, 12–13
Ear tufts, 12–13, 45
Eggs, 22–3
Elf Owl, 20, 42
Eyes, 9, 10–12

Facial discs, 13
Falconiformes, 9–10
Feathers, 7–8, 13, 15
Feeding of young, 23–4, 25, 34
Fish owls, 36–7, 39; Malaysian Fish, 37, 39; Pel's Fishing, 36, 39
Flight, silent, 13, 15; of the young, 25
Food storing, 31

Hawk owls, 39; Barking, 39; Boobook, 38; Hawk, 39; Powerful, 39
Hooting, *see* Voice
Hunting techniques, by sight, 11–12, 36, 39; by sound, 13, 15

Incubation, 21, 22–3

Little owls, 40; Burrowing, 20, 22, 40, 41; Little, 40

Mating, 19–20
Migration, 16
Mobbing, 18–19

Nests, 20–2

Owlets, 22, 23–4, 25

Pairing, 19
Pellets, 24–5, 40
Persecution, of Barn Owl, 27
Pygmy owls, 40; Eurasian Pygmy, 40, 42; Ferruginous Pygmy, 6

Roosting, 18

Scops owls, 29–31; European Scops, 16, 30, 31; White-faced Scops,
   8, 31
Screech owls, 31; Common Screech, 31
Sexual display, 19
Snowy Owl, 34, 35
Strigiformes, 10
Survival of species, 23, 25, 46

Talons, 9, 10, 36
Territory, 16–17, 18
Threat display, 16, 17–18, 35

Voice, 17, 19

Wood owls, 43–4; Great Grey, 6, 20, 43; Tawny, 12, 15, 16, 17, 19,
   20, 24, 43, 44